MEDITATIONS

OF

HENRY
DAVID
THOREAU

A Light
in the Woods

MEDITATIONS
OF
HENRY
DAVID
THOREAU

A Light
in the Woods

Compiled and edited by
CHRIS HIGHLAND

 WILDERNESS PRESS · BERKELEY, CA

1st EDITION December 2002
  2nd printing July 2003
  3rd printing January 2004
  4th printing March 2005

Book and cover design by Larry B. Van Dyke
Photographs by C. Highland except where otherwise noted
Cover photos: *Henry David Thoreau* courtesy of the Library
              of Congress; *Vine Maples, Moonset Sunrise* and
              Winter White (regal robes) © 2002 C. Highland
Frontispiece photo: *Henry David Thoreau* courtesy of the
              Collections of the Thoreau Society at the
              Thoreau Institute at Walden Woods

Library of Congress Card Number 2003041156
ISBN 0-89997-321-3
UPC 7-19609-97321-8

Manufactured in the United States of America
Published by: **Wilderness Press**
               1200 5th Street
               Berkeley, CA 94710
               (800) 443-7227; FAX (510) 558-1696
               mail@wildernesspress.com
               www.wildernesspress.com

               Contact us for a free catalog

Library of Congress Cataloging-in-Publication Data

Thoreau, Henry David, 1817–1862.
    Meditations of Henry David Thoreau : a light in the woods / compiled and edited by
Chris Highland.—1st ed.
        p. cm.
    Includes bibliographical references.
    ISBN 0-89997-321-3
    1. Nature. 2. Meditations. 3. Thoreau, Henry David, 1817–1862. I. Highland, Chris,
1955– II. Title.

QH81.T612 2004
508—dc21

                                        2003041156

Introduction

"I believed that the woods were not tenantless, but chokefull of honest spirits as good as myself any day — not an empty chamber, in which chemistry was left to work alone, but an inhabited house — and for a few moments I enjoyed fellowship with them."[1]

~ Henry David Thoreau
Maine Woods

When he adventured into the Maine Woods in 1846, the 29-year old honest spirit Henry David Thoreau had already been a tenant at Walden Pond in Massachusetts for a year (since July 4th, 1845). The deeper, "inhabited house" of the north woods enticed him to deepen the spiritually-guided botany that characterized his life. He sought the extraordinary in the common and he found it. There, as everywhere, he felt something present that the civil world, the village, couldn't see, hear, or feel. He opened himself to taste what he would later call "the flavor of life." A flavor one can only savor when "obeying the suggestions of a higher light within."[2]

One evening, after noticing an eerie glow in a dead log deep in those Maine backwoods, he investigated the natural phosphorescence and remarked that he had given scant thought "that there was such a light shining in the darkness of the wilderness for me." He concluded that he had more to learn from the forest and its inhabitants — including

the Native peoples who held their own light — than from any wisdom he carried along. It was a liminal moment for him — a threshold illuminated with wild, blood-swirling mystery.

Thoreau (rhymes with *furrow*) is one of those eminently quotable persons in American history who seemed to have plowed himself into the landscape of the New World. His eye was trained on the ever-renewing fecundity of worlds at his feet. Collecting his thoughts is, for us, a kind of inner-farming — tilling, hoeing, harvesting the heartland of his, and our, richly American home. As his former housemate and devoted colleague Ralph Waldo Emerson eulogized, "His eye was open to beauty, and his ear to music. He found these, not in rare conditions, but wheresoever he went."[3] His legacy is a lasting map into Beauty.

Thoreau walked into the natural world and felt the world walk into him. Emerson recalled Thoreau saying he could find his path in the woods at night "better by [my] feet than [my] eyes."[4] Fiercely independent yet welcoming enlightened human society, he constantly went to the forest for the inspiring companionship of "kindred" Nature. There he found, again in Emerson's words, that his closeness with Nature "inspired his friends with curiosity to see the world through his eyes, and to hear his adventures."[5]

His insight resounded into the twentieth century, *spiriting the activism* of shakers like Mahatma Gandhi and Martin Luther King, Jr. and *activating the spirit* of movers like Sigurd Olson and Dorothee Soelle. What Thoreau saw with his eyes and felt with his feet continue to kindle a lamp for the walk of new generations.

In Henry David Thoreau our modern eye can see a new light. His lucent wisdom warms a rich and sprouting garden of earthy spirituality composted

with a keen sense of scientific and philosophical investigation. Thoreau models a specially balanced inquisitive mind that integrates the most profound discoveries of the heart and soul. He embodied the traits of both preservationist and religion professor. He personalized an exciting and fresh paradigm for a symbiosis of related disciplines including philosophy and ecology—a relationship that remains today both rare and sorely needed. Thoreau's intimacy with the world at his feet touched his hands, his head, his whole being and sunk in. This is best illustrated by his delight in digging into the earth, literally and figuratively, turning over rich soil for reflection and introspection. Because he knew he was made of that earth, he could open himself to the mystery just under the surface, revealed by Nature's playful and parental care. "Perhaps Nature would condescend to make use of us even without our knowledge, as when we help to scatter her seeds in our walks, and carry burs [sic] and cockles on our clothes from field to field."[6] The baggy-pants botanist may not have known it, but his clothes bore wondrous seeds for future planting and reaping.

A Light in the Woods is arranged to suggest pilgrimage. We join Thoreau along with poets, writers, spiritual guides, shamans and saints, to saunter as sojourners deeper into Nature's miracles. When I first walked alongside Henry in college I knew that he would be with me for years ahead. Every essay or poem inspired me to write and be present in my daily life and yet to remember that words alone cannot express the depths of the heart. For that class at the university I memorized a simple line that stays with me still: "My life has been the poem I would have writ. But I could not both live and utter it."[7] I believe this is what the great teachers meant when they urged an awareness of the Word beneath the

words, the Way beyond the path, the Torah or Gospel hidden near at hand, behind the awe-filled silences that mark moments of being human.

This book is a companion for you to carry with open curiosity into the beauties and wonders of the new worlds around you. Thoreau, like Emerson, like Muir in other woods, whittled a down-to-earth philosophical spirituality in the woods of New England. No matter where we live or journey, his roots are ours. And as we find our own Waldens, we can ask the same question Henry asked on the shore of the pond, "Why has humanity rooted itself thus firmly in the earth, but that it may rise in the same proportion into the heavens above?"[8] We are rising, and as we lift our spirit, we can bow in gratitude for the Concord pilgrim's wisdom. "Heaven is under our feet, as well as over our heads."[9] Looking down or looking up, his words seed and water our inner land, and we rise fresh and renewed.

Thoreau's wisdom can be tasted like tea by a mountain lake and inspire days and nights as you saunter through sunlight or moonglow. Let him be a trusted companion, in all places where we hear the one calling out in the wilderness—the young, noble soul who, like the prophets of ancient times, found a strange and special spiritual light in the wildest places of his native land.

~ *Chris Highland,*
Fall 2002

"The soul is a lamp whose light is steady,
for it burns in a shelter where no winds come."

~ *Bhagavad Gita*

Notes to the Introduction

1. *The Maine Woods*. Boston: Shambhala, 1995, p. 83.
2. *Wild Fruits*. N.Y.: Norton, 2000, p. 166.
3. "Thoreau," in *The Writings of Ralph Waldo Emerson*. N.Y.: Random House, 1950, pp. 907-908.
4. Ibid., p. 900-901.
5. Ibid., p. 911.
6. "A Week on the Concord and Merrimack Rivers," in *The Portable Thoreau*, edited by Carl Bode. NY: Viking, 1977, p. 223.
7. "Journal," Ibid., p. 27.
8. "Economy," from *Walden*, Ibid., p. 271.
9. "The Pond In Winter," from *Walden*, Ibid., p. 525.

A Note on Inclusive Language

It is evident to me that Thoreau clearly intended a universal understanding in his writings, even as he employed the common terminology of his day, including the use of the male gender to stand for all of humankind.

While I believe that changing Thoreau's gendered pronouns and nouns would actually amplify Thoreau's voice for the 21st century and remove obstacles that some readers may encounter in reading these selections as spiritual meditations, I have represented Thoreau in his own words and presented these quotations accurately and wholly.

I ask the reader to keep these concerns in mind when reading these pages, and encourage you to substitute the inclusive wording yourself. I believe that Henry David Thoreau, the visionary and egalitarian human being, would appreciate that.

Contents

"Therefore, as doth the pilgrim,
whom the night hastes darkly
to imprison on the way,
Think on thy home, my soul,
and think aright
Of what's yet left thee
of life's wasting day:
Thy sun posts westward,
passed is thy morn,
And twice it is not given thee
to be born."

~ Henry David Thoreau
from "A Week on the Concord and Merrimack Rivers"

In Honor Of

The Highland Brothers
Paul, Robert, Howard and Warren
&
For companions
who hike the higher lands
and climb the trees

1

Morning Air

The indescribable innocence and beneficence of Nature—of sun and wind and rain, of summer and winter—such health, such cheer, they afford forever! and such sympathy have they ever with our race, that all Nature would be affected, and the sun's brightness fade, and the winds would sigh humanely, and the clouds rain tears, and the woods shed their leaves and put on mourning in midsummer, if any man should ever for a just cause grieve. Shall I not have intelligence with the earth? Am I not partly leaves and vegetable mould myself?

What is the pill which will keep us well, serene, contented? Not my or thy great-grandfather's, but our great-grandmother Nature's universal, vegetable, botanic medicines, by which she has kept herself young always. . . . For my panacea . . . let me have a draught of undiluted morning air. Morning air! If men will not drink of this at the fountainhead of the day, why, then, we must even bottle up some and sell it in the shops, for the benefit of those who have lost their subscription ticket to morning time in this world.

"Each morning,
The glory of breaking light,
of the sun on fire,
and from its flaming light,
creation's garden is born."

~ Bob King
Strings of Light

2

Winter Warmth

In winter we lead a more inward life. Our hearts are warm and cheery, like cottages under drifts, whose windows and doors are half concealed, but from whose chimneys the smoke cheerfully ascends. . . . We enjoy now, not an Oriental, but a Boreal leisure, around warm stoves and fireplaces, and watch the shadow of motes in the sunbeams.

Sometimes our fate grows too homely and familiarly serious ever to be cruel. Consider how for three months the human destiny is wrapped in furs. The good Hebrew Revelation takes no cognizance of all this cheerful snow. Is there no religion for the temperate and frigid zones? We know of no scripture which records the pure benignity of the gods on a New England winter night. The best scripture, after all, records but a meager faith. Its saints live reserved and austere. Let a brave, devout one spend the year in the woods of Maine or Labrador, and see if the Hebrew Scriptures speak adequately to their condition and experience, from the setting in of winter to the breaking up of the ice.

*"The light is short-lived and
never twice the same,
yet it always says 'December'."*

~ Robert Michael Pyle
Wintergreen

3

Acorn & Chestnut

I was not born to be forced. I will breathe after my own fashion. Let us see who is the strongest. What force has a multitude? They only can force me who obey a higher law than I. They force me to become like themselves. I do not hear of men being forced to live this way or that by masses of men. What sort of life were that to live? When I meet a government which says to me, "Your money or your life," why should I be in haste to give it my money? It may be in a great strait, and not know what to do: I cannot help that. It must help itself; do as I do. It is not worth the while to snivel about it. I am not responsible for the successful working of the machinery of society. I am not the son of the engineer. I perceive that, when an acorn and a chestnut fall side by side, the one does not remain inert to make way for the other, but both obey their own laws, and spring and grow and flourish as best they can, till one, perchance, overshadows and destroys the other. If a plant cannot live according to its nature, it dies; and so a man.

*"No law can be sacred to me
but that of my nature."*

~ Ralph W. Emerson
Self-Reliance

4

Streams of Truth

They who know of no purer sources of truth, who have traced up its stream no higher, stand, and wisely stand, by the Bible and the Constitution, and drink at it there with reverence and humility; but they who behold where it comes trickling into this lake or that pool, gird up their loins once more, and continue their pilgrimage toward its fountainhead.

*"We are caught in an inescapable
network of mutuality,
tied in a single garment of destiny."*

~ Martin Luther King, Jr.
Letter from a Birmingham Jail

5

A Light in the Woods

Getting up some time after midnight to collect the scattered brands together, while my companions were sound asleep, I observed, partly in the fire, which had ceased to blaze, a perfectly regular elliptical ring of light, about five inches in its shortest diameter, six or seven in its longer, and from one eighth to one quarter of an inch wide. . . . I saw at once that it must be phosphorescent wood, which I had so often heard of, but never chanced to see. . . .

I was exceedingly interested in this phenomenon, and already felt paid for my journey. It could hardly have thrilled me more if it had taken the form of letters, or of the human face. If I had met with this ring of light while groping in this forest alone, away from any fire, I should have been still more surprised. I little thought that there was such a light shining in the darkness of the wilderness for me. . . .

I did not regret my not having seen this before, since I now saw it under circumstances so favorable. I was in just the frame of mind to see something wonderful. . . . It suggested to me that there was something to be seen if one had eyes. It made a believer of me more than before. I believed that the woods were not tenantless, but chokefull of honest spirits as good as myself any day—not an empty chamber, in which chemistry was left to work alone, but an inhabited house—and for a few moments I enjoyed fellowship with them.

"[The outdoor meditator dwells in] compassionate love. . .
by the perception of light."

~ Gautama Buddha
Pali Canon

6

Floating on Life's Current

The Mississippi, the Ganges, and the Nile, those journeying atoms from the Rocky Mountains, the Himmaleh, and Mountains of the Moon, have a kind of personal importance in the annals of the world. The heavens are not yet drained over their sources, but the Mountains of the Moon still send their annual tribute to the Pasha without fail, as they did to the Pharaohs, though he must collect the rest of his revenue at the point of the sword. Rivers must have been the guides which conducted the footsteps of the first travelers. They are the constant lure, when they flow by our doors, to distant enterprise and adventure; and, by a natural impulse, the dwellers on their banks will at length accompany their currents to the lowlands of the globe, or explore at their invitation the interior of continents. They are the natural highways of all nations, not only leveling the ground and removing obstacles from the path of the traveler, quenching his thirst, and bearing him on their bosoms, but conducting him through the most interesting scenery, the most populous portions of the globe, and where the animal and vegetable kingdoms attain their greatest perfection.

I had often stood on the banks of the Concord, watching the lapse of the current, an emblem of all progress, following the same law with the system, with time, and all that is made; the weeds at the bottom gently bending down the stream, shaken by the watery wind, still planted where their seeds had sunk, but ere long to die and go down likewise; the shining pebbles, not yet anxious to better their condition, the chips and weeds, and occasional logs and stems of trees, that floated past, fulfilling their fate, were objects of singular interest to me, and at last I resolved to launch myself on its bosom, and float whither it would bear me.

*"For the raindrop,
joy is in entering the river."*

~ Ghalib
quoted by Stephen Mitchell in *The Enlightened Heart*

7

Nature Adorned

Gradually the village murmur subsided, and we seemed to be embarked on the placid current of our dreams, floating from past to future as silently as one awakes to fresh morning or evening thoughts. . . .

From the more distant waysides, which we occasionally passed, and banks where the sun had lodged, was reflected still a dull yellow beam from the ranks of tansy, now past its prime. In short, Nature seemed to have adorned herself for our departure with a profusion of fringes and curls, mingled with the bright tints of flowers, reflected in the water. But we missed the white water-lily, which is the queen of river flowers, its reign being over for this season. He makes his voyage too late, perhaps, by a true water clock who delays so long. Many of this species inhabit our Concord water. I have passed down the river before sunrise on a summer morning between fields of lilies still shut in sleep; and when, at length, the flakes of sunlight from over the bank fell on the surface of the water, whole fields of white blossoms seemed to flash open before me, as I floated along, like the unfolding of a banner, so sensible is this flower to the influence of the sun's rays.

"Now I know what it is to sit enthroned amid the clouds of sunset."

~ Rudyard Kipling
Tour Through Yellowstone

8

Night by a River

To the right and left, as far as the horizon, were straggling pine woods with their plumes against the sky, and across the river were rugged hills, covered with shrub oaks, tangled with grape-vines and ivy, with here and there a gray rock jutting out from the maze. The sides of these cliffs, though a quarter of a mile distant, were almost heard to rustle while we looked at them, it was such a leafy wilderness; a place for fauns and satyrs, and where bats hung all day to the rocks, and at evening flitted over the water, and fireflies husbanded their light under the grass and leaves against the night. When we had pitched our tent on the hillside, a few rods from the shore, we sat looking through its triangular door in the twilight at our lonely mast on the shore just seen above the alders, and hardly yet come to a standstill from the swaying of the stream; the first encroachment of commerce on this land. There was our port, our Ostia. That straight, geometrical line against the water and the sky stood for the last refinements of civilized life, and what of sublimity there is in history was there symbolized.

*"I will go to the bank by the wood
and become undisguised and naked,
I am mad for it to be in contact with me."*

~ Walt Whitman
Song of Myself

9

Tree Shelter

When compelled by a shower to take shelter under a tree, we may improve that opportunity for a more minute inspection of some of Nature's works. I have stood under a tree in the woods half a day at a time, during a heavy rain in the summer, and yet employed myself happily and profitably there prying with microscopic eye into the crevices of the bark or the leaves or the fungi at my feet. "Riches are the attendants of the miser; and the heavens rain plenteously upon the mountains." I can fancy that it would be a luxury to stand up to one's chin in some retired swamp a whole summer day, scenting the wild honeysuckle and bilberry blows, and lulled by the minstrelsy of gnats and mosquitoes! A day passed in the society of those Greek sages, such as described in the Banquet of Xenophon, would not be comparable with the dry wet of decayed cranberry vines, and the fresh Attic salt of the moss-beds. Say twelve hours of genial and familiar converse with the leopard frog; the sun to rise behind alder and dogwood, and climb buoyantly to his meridian of two hands' breadth, and finally sink to rest behind some bold western hummock. To hear the evening chant of the mosquito from a thousand green chapels, and the bittern begin to boom from some concealed fort like a sunset gun! Surely one may as profitably be soaked in the juices of a swamp for one day as pick his way dry-shod over sand. Cold and damp—are they not as rich experience as warmth and dryness?

"The darkest scriptures of the mountains are illumined with bright passages of love."

~John Muir
Mountains of California

10

To Travel Always

The cheapest way to travel, and the way to travel the furthest in the shortest distance, is to go afoot, carrying a dipper, a spoon, and a fish-line, some Indian meal, some salt, and some sugar. When you come to a brook or pond, you can catch fish and cook them; or you can boil a hasty-pudding; or you can buy a loaf of bread at a farmer's house for fourpence, moisten it in the next brook that crosses the road, and dip it into your sugar—this alone will last you a whole day—or, if you are accustomed to heartier living, you can buy a quart of milk for two cents, crumb your bread or cold pudding into it, and eat it with your own spoon out of your own dish. Any one of these things I mean, not all together. I have traveled thus some hundreds of miles without taking any meal in a house, sleeping on the ground when convenient, and found it cheaper, and in many respects more profitable, than staying at home. So that some have inquired why it would not be best to travel always. But I never thought of traveling simply as a means of getting a livelihood. . . . The traveler must be born again on the road, and earn a passport from the elements, the principal powers that be for him.

*"To get close to the earth and see the stars —
this is travel."*

~ Mary Roberts Rinehart
Rockies

11

The Art of God

The works of man are everywhere swallowed up in the immensity of nature. . . . Nature is prepared to welcome into her scenery the finest work of human art, for she is herself an art so cunning that the artist never appears in his work.

Art is not tame, and Nature is not wild, in the ordinary sense. A perfect work of man's art would also be wild or natural in a good sense. Man tames Nature only that he may at last make her more free even than he found her, though he may never yet have succeeded. . . .

As we have said, Nature is a greater and more perfect art, the art of God; though, referred to herself, she is genius; and there is a similarity between her operations and man's art even in the details and trifles. When the overhanging pine drops into the water, by the sun and water, and the wind rubbing it against the shore, its boughs are worn into fantastic shapes, and white and smooth, as if turned in a lathe. Man's art has wisely imitated those forms into which all matter is most inclined to run, as foliage and fruit. A hammock swung in a grove assumes the exact form of a canoe, broader or narrower, and higher or lower at the ends, as more or fewer persons are in it, and it rolls in the air with the motion of the body, like a canoe in the water. Our art leaves its shavings and its dust about; her art exhibits itself even in the shavings and the dust which we make. She has perfected herself by an eternity of practice.

"From art, from nature, from the schools,
Let random influences glance,
Like light in many a shiver'd lance,
That breaks about the dappled pools."

~Alfred Lord Tennyson
In Memoriam A.H.H.

12

A Stronger Light

Every man casts a shadow; not his body only, but his imperfectly mingled spirit. This is his grief. Let him turn which way he will, it falls opposite to the sun; short at noon, long at eve. Did you never see it? But, referred to the sun, it is widest at its base, which is no greater than his capacity. The divine light is diffused almost entirely around us, and by means of the refraction of light, or else by a certain self-luminousness, or, as some will have it, transparency, if we preserve ourselves untarnished, we are able to enlighten our shaded side. At any rate, our darkest grief has that bronze color of the moon eclipsed. There is no ill which may not be dissipated, like the dark, if you let in a stronger light upon it. Shadows, referred to the source of light, are pyramids whose bases are never greater than those of the substances which cast them, but light is a spherical congeries of pyramids, whose very apexes are the sun itself, and hence the system shines with uninterrupted light. But if the light we use is but a paltry and narrow taper, most objects will cast a shadow wider than themselves.

*"You have caused a new light
to shine in our hearts."*

~ Book of Common Prayer
Epiphany

13

Out of Doors

In summer we live out of doors, and have only impulses and feelings, which are all for action, and must wait commonly for the stillness and longer nights of autumn and winter before any thought will subside; we are sensible that behind the rustling leaves, and the stacks of grain, and the bare clusters of the grape, there is the field of a wholly new life, which no man has lived; that even this earth was made for more mysterious and nobler inhabitants than men and women. In the hues of October sunsets, we see the portals to other mansions than those which we occupy, not far off geographically,

There is a place beyond that flaming hill,
From whence the stars their thin appearance shed,
A place beyond all place, where never ill,
Nor impure thought was ever harbored.

Sometimes a mortal feels in himself Nature—not his Father but his Mother stirs within him, and he becomes immortal with her immortality. From time to time she claims kindredship with us, and some globule from her veins steals up into our own.

*"I wonder at all the things
I think I've touched but haven't."*

~ Barry Lopez
Crossing Open Ground

14

Portals of Nature

It is easier to discover another such a new world as Columbus did, than to go within one fold of this which we appear to know so well; the land is lost sight of, the compass varies, and mankind mutiny; and still history accumulates like rubbish before the portals of nature. But there is only necessary a moment's sanity and sound senses, to teach us that there is a nature behind the ordinary, in which we have only some vague pre-emption right and western reserve as yet. We live on the outskirts of that region. Carved wood, and floating boughs, and sunset skies are all that we know of it. We are not to be imposed on by the longest spell of weather. Let us not, my friends, be wheedled and cheated into good behavior to earn the salt of our eternal porridge, whoever they are that attempt it. Let us wait a little, and not purchase any clearing here, trusting that richer bottoms will soon be put up. It is but thin soil where we stand; I have felt my roots in a richer ere this. I have seen a bunch of violets in a glass vase, tied loosely with a straw, which reminded me of myself. . . .

Thus thoughtfully we were rowing homeward to find some autumnal work to do, and help on the revolution of the seasons. Perhaps Nature would condescend to make use of us even without our knowledge, as when we help to scatter her seeds in our walks, and carry burs and cockles on our clothes from field to field.

*"Seeds — all were somehow triumphing
over life's limitations."*

~ Loren Eiseley
The Immense Journey

15

Silence

As we looked up in silence to those distant lights, we were reminded that it was a rare imagination which first taught that the stars are worlds, and had conferred a great benefit on mankind. It is recorded in the Chronicle of Bernaldez that in Columbus' first voyage the natives "pointed towards the heavens, making signs that they believed that there was all power and holiness." We have reason to be grateful for celestial phenomena, for they chiefly answer to the ideal in man. The stars are distant and unobtrusive, but bright and enduring as our fairest and most memorable experiences. "Let the immortal depth of your soul lead you, but earnestly extend your eyes upwards."

As the truest society approaches always nearer to solitude, so the most excellent speech finally falls into Silence. Silence is audible to all men at all times, and in all places. She is when we hear inwardly, sound when we hear outwardly. Creation has not displaced her, but is her visible framework and foil. All sounds are her servants, and purveyors, proclaiming not only that their mistress is, but is a rare mistress, and earnestly to be sought after. They are so far akin to Silence that they are but bubbles on her surface, which straightway burst, and evidence of the strength and prolificness of the undercurrent; a faint utterance of Silence, and then only agreeable to our auditory nerves when they contrast themselves with and relieve the former. In proportion as they do this, and are heighteners and intensifiers of the Silence, they are harmony and purest melody.

Silence is the universal refuge. . . .

"There was little conversation,
for an impressive scene overawed speech."

~ Mark Twain
Hawaii

16

Sacred Forests & City Caves

I was impressed by the quiet religious atmosphere of the [Notre Dame cathedral in Montreal]. It was a great cave in the midst of a city; and what were the altars and the tinsel but the sparkling stalactites, into which you entered in a moment, and where the still atmosphere and the somber light disposed to serious and profitable thought? Such a cave at hand, which you can enter any day, is worth a thousand of our churches which are open only on Sundays—hardly long enough for an airing—and then filled with a bustling congregation. A church where the priest is the least part, where you do your own preaching, where the universe preaches to you and can be heard. . . .

In Concord, to be sure, we do not need such. Our forests are such a church, far grander and more sacred. We dare not leave *our* meetinghouses open for fear they would be profaned. Such a cave, such a shrine, in one of our groves, for instance, how long would it be respected—for what purposes would it be entered, by such baboons as we are? I think of its value not only to religion, but to philosophy and to poetry; besides a reading-room, to have a thinking-room in every city! Perchance the time will come when every house even will have not only its sleeping-rooms, and dining-room, and talking-room or parlor, but its thinking-room also, and the architects will put it into their plans. Let it be furnished and ornamented with whatever conduces to serious and creative thought. I should not object to the holy water, or any other simple symbol, if it were consecrated by the imagination of the worshipers. . . .

As for the Protestant churches, here or elsewhere, they did not interest me, for it is only as caves that churches interest me at all, and in that respect they were inferior.

"Seek only there
Where the grey light meets the green air
The hermit's chapel, the pilgrim's prayer."

~ T.S. Eliot
Usk

17

Ploughed into the Soil

I see young men, my townsmen, whose misfortune it is to have inherited farms, houses, barns, cattle, and farming tools; for these are more easily acquired than got rid of. Better if they had been born in the open pasture and suckled by a wolf, that they might have seen with clearer eyes what field they were called to labor in. Who made them serfs of the soil? Why should they eat their sixty acres, when man is condemned to eat only his peck of dirt? Why should they begin digging their graves as soon as they are born? They have got to live a man's life, pushing all these things before them, and get on as well as they can. How many a poor immortal soul have I met well nigh crushed and smothered under its load, creeping down the road of life, pushing before it a barn seventy-five feet by forty, its Augean stables never cleansed, and one hundred acres of land, tillage, mowing, pasture, and wood-lot! The portion-less, who struggle with no such unnecessary inherited encumbrances, find it labor enough to subdue and cultivate a few cubic feet of flesh.

But men labor under a mistake. The better part of the man is soon ploughed into the soil for compost. By a seeming fate, commonly called necessity, they are employed, as it says in an old book, laying up treasures which moth and rust will corrupt and thieves break through and steal. It is a fool's life, as they will find when they get to the end of it, if not before. . . .

Most men, even in this comparatively free country, through mere ignorance and mistake, are so occupied with the factitious cares and superfluously coarse labors of life that its finer fruits cannot be plucked by them.

"I firmly believe that nature brings solace in all troubles."

~Anne Frank
Diary of Anne Frank

18

The Wise Choice

As if you could kill time without injuring eternity.

The mass of men lead lives of quiet desperation. What is called resignation is confirmed desperation. From the desperate city you go into the desperate country, and have to console yourself with the bravery of minks and muskrats. A stereotyped but unconscious despair is concealed even under what are called the games and amusements of mankind. There is no play in them, for this comes after work. But it is a characteristic of wisdom not to do desperate things.

When we consider what, to use the words of the catechism, is the chief end of man, and what are the true necessaries and means of life, it appears as if men had deliberately chosen the common mode of living because they preferred it to any other. Yet they honestly think there is no choice left. But alert and healthy natures remember that the sun rose clear. It is never too late to give up our prejudices. No way of thinking or doing, however ancient, can be trusted without proof. What everybody echoes or in silence passes by as true today may turn out to be false-hood tomorrow, mere smoke of opinion, which some had trusted for a cloud that would sprinkle fertilizing rain on their fields.

*"Open your inmost chamber
and light its lamp."*

~ Mirabai
quoted by Andrew Harvey in *The Essential Mystics*

19

A Greater Miracle

We might try our lives by a thousand simple tests; as, for instance, that the same sun which ripens my beans illumines at once a system of earths like ours. If I had remembered this it would have prevented some mistakes. This was not the light in which I hoed them. The stars are the apexes of what wonderful triangles! What distant and different beings in the various mansions of the universe are contemplating the same one at the same moment! Nature and human life are as various as our several constitutions. Who shall say what prospect life offers to another? Could a greater miracle take place than for us to look through each other's eyes for an instant? We should live in all the ages of the world in an hour; ay, in all the worlds of the ages. History, Poetry, Mythology!—I know of no reading of another's experience so startling and informing as this would be. . . .

So thoroughly and sincerely are we compelled to live, reverencing our life, and denying the possibility of change. This is the only way, we say; but there are as many ways as there can be drawn radii from one center. All change is a miracle to contemplate; but it is a miracle which is taking place every instant.

*"A good heart, a heart like the earth,
which drinks up the rain that falls on it
and yields a rich harvest."*

~ Gregory of Nyssa
quoted by Kathleen Norris in *Dakota*

20

Comforts of Life

Most of the luxuries, and many of the so-called comforts of life, are not only not indispensable, but positive hindrances to the elevation of mankind. With respect to luxuries and comforts, the wisest have ever lived a more simple and meager life than the poor. The ancient philosophers, Chinese, Hindu, Persian, and Greek, were a class than which none has been poorer in outward riches, none so rich in inward. We know not much about them. It is remarkable that *we* know so much of them as we do. The same is true of the more modern reformers and benefactors of their race. None can be an impartial or wise observer of human life but from the vantage ground of what *we* should call voluntary poverty. Of a life of luxury the fruit is luxury, whether in agriculture, or commerce, or literature, or art. There are nowadays professors of philosophy, but not philosophers. Yet it is admirable to profess because it was once admirable to live. To be a philosopher is not merely to have subtle thoughts, nor even to found a school, but so to love wisdom as to live according to its dictates, a life of simplicity, independence, magnanimity, and trust.

"The whole world was a nest on its humble tilt, in the maze of the universe, holding us."

~ Linda Hogan
Dwellings

21

Nick of Time

In any weather, at any hour of the day or night, I have been anxious to improve the nick of time, and notch it on my stick too; to stand on the meeting of two eternities, the past and future, which is precisely the present moment; to toe that line. You will pardon some obscurities, for there are more secrets in my trade than in most men's, and yet not voluntarily kept, but inseparable from its very nature. I would gladly tell all that I know about it, and never paint "No Admittance" on my gate. . . .

To anticipate, not the sunrise and the dawn merely, but, if possible, Nature herself! How many mornings, summer and winter, before yet any neighbor was stirring about his business, have I been about mine! No doubt, many of my townsmen have met me returning from this enterprise, farmers starting for Boston in the twilight, or woodchoppers going to their work. It is true, I never assisted the sun materially in his rising, but, doubt not, it was of the last importance only to be present at it.

*"In the spiritual field where she sowed,
the weather was always right."*

~ Hymn to Saint Brigid
quoted by Robert Van De Weyer in *Celtic Fire*

22

Face to the Woods

The life which men praise and regard as successful is but one kind. Why should we exaggerate any one kind at the expense of the others?

Finding that my fellow-citizens were not likely to offer me any room in the courthouse, or any curacy or living anywhere else, but I must shift for myself, I turned my face more exclusively than ever to the woods, where I was better known. I determined to go into business at once, and not wait to acquire the usual capital, using such slender means as I had already got. My purpose in going to Walden Pond was not to live cheaply nor to live dearly there, but to transact some private business with the fewest obstacles; to be hindered from accomplishing which for want of a little common sense, a little enterprise and business talent, appeared not so sad as foolish.

"The hardest and the most significant work is going to be the work each one of us does on ourselves."

~ Elizabeth Lesser
The New American Spirituality

23

New Clothes

A man who has at length found something to do will not need to get a new suit to do it in; for him the old will do, that has lain dusty in the garret for an indeterminate period. Old shoes will serve a hero longer than they have served his valet—if a hero ever has a valet—bare feet are older than shoes, and he can make them do. Only they who go to soirées and legislative halls must have new coats, coats to change as often as the man changes in them. But if my jacket and trousers, my hat and shoes, are fit to worship God in, they will do; will they not? Who ever saw his old clothes—his old coat, actually worn out, resolved into its primitive elements, so that it was not a deed of charity to bestow it on some poorer boy, by him perchance to be bestowed on some poorer still, or shall we say richer, who could do with less? I say, beware of all enterprises that require new clothes, and not rather a new wearer of clothes. If there is not a new man, how can the new clothes be made to fit? If you have any enterprise before you, try it in your old clothes. All men want, not something to *do with*, but something to *do*, or rather something to *be*. Perhaps we should never procure a new suit, however ragged or

dirty the old, until we have so conducted, so enter-
prised or sailed in some way, that we feel like new
men in the old, and that to retain it would be like
keeping new wine in old bottles.

"The really important thing
is not to live,
but to live well."

~ Socrates
Crito

24

Sojourner in Nature

The very simplicity and nakedness of man's life in the primitive ages imply this advantage, at least, that they left him still but a sojourner in nature. When he was refreshed with food and sleep he contemplated his journey again. He dwelt, as it were, in a tent in this world, and was either threading the valleys, or crossing the plains, or climbing the mountain tops. But lo! men have become the tools of their tools. The man who independently plucked the fruits when he was hungry is become a farmer; and he who stood under a tree for shelter, a housekeeper. We now no longer camp as for a night, but have settled down on earth and forgotten heaven. . . .

Before we can adorn our houses with beautiful objects the walls must be stripped, and our lives must be stripped, and beautiful housekeeping and beautiful living be laid for a foundation: now, a taste for the beautiful is most cultivated out of doors, where there is no house and no housekeeper. . . .

Not that all architectural ornament is to be neg-
lected even in the rudest periods; but let our houses
first be lined with beauty, where they come in contact with our lives, like the tenement of the shellfish,
and not overlaid with it. But alas! I have been inside
one or two of them, and know what they are lined
with.

"And they shall go into the wilderness
to prepare the way."

~ Qumran Community Rule
Dead Sea Scrolls

25

Friend of the Pine

So I went on for some days cutting and hewing timber, and also studs and rafters, all with my narrow axe, not having many communicable or scholar-like thoughts, singing to myself, —

Men say they know many things;
But lo! they have taken wings —
The arts and sciences,
And a thousand appliances:
The wind that blows
Is all that anybody knows.

I hewed the main timbers six inches square, most of the studs on two sides only, and the rafters and floor timbers on one side, leaving the rest of the bark on, so that they were just as straight and much stronger than sawed ones. Each stick was carefully mortised or tenoned by its stump, for I had borrowed other tools by this time. My days in the woods were not very long ones; yet I usually carried my dinner of bread and butter, and read the newspaper in which it was wrapped, at noon, sitting amid the green pine boughs which I had cut off, and to my bread was imparted some of their fragrance, for my hands were covered with a thick coat of pitch. Before I had done I was more the friend than the foe of the pine tree, though I had cut down some of them, having become better acquainted with it. Sometimes a rambler in the wood was attracted by the sound of my axe, and we chatted pleasantly over the chips which I had made.

By the middle of April, for I made no haste in my work, but rather made the most of it, my house was framed and ready for the raising.

*"This thought of enlightenment
is a tree of rest for the wearied world
journeying on the road of being."*

~ Shantideva
quoted by Andrew Harvey in *The Essential Mystics*

26

Neighbor to the Birds

This was an airy and unplastered cabin, fit to entertain a traveling god, and where a goddess might trail her garments. The winds which passed over my dwelling were such as sweep over the ridges of mountains, bearing the broken strains, or celestial parts only, of terrestrial music. The morning wind forever blows, the poem of creation is uninterrupted; but few are the ears that hear it. Olympus is but the outside of the earth everywhere.

The only house I had been the owner of before, if I except a boat, was a tent, which I used occasionally when making excursions in the summer, and this is still rolled up in my garret; but the boat, after passing from hand to hand, has gone down the stream of time. With this more substantial shelter about me, I had made some progress toward settling in the world. This frame, so slightly clad, was a sort of crystallization around me, and reacted on the builder. It was suggestive somewhat as a picture in outlines. I did not need to go outdoors to take the air, for the atmosphere within had lost none of its freshness. It was not so much within doors as behind a door where I sat, even in the rainiest weather. The Harivansa says, "An abode without birds is like a meat without seasoning." Such was not my abode, for I found myself suddenly neighbor to the birds; not by having imprisoned one, but having caged myself near them.

"Remember, remember
the sacredness of things
running streams and dwellings
the young within the nest
a hearth for sacred fire
the holy flame of fire."

~ Pawnee prayer
quoted by Ursula Goodenough in *The Sacred Depths of Nature*

27

To Be Awake is to Be Alive

Morning is when I am awake and there is a dawn in me. Moral reform is the effort to throw off sleep. Why is it that men give so poor an account of their day if they have not been slumbering? They are not such poor calculators. If they had not been overcome with drowsiness, they would have performed something. The millions are awake enough for physical labor; but only one in a million is awake enough for effective intellectual exertion, only one in a hundred millions to a poetic or divine life. To be awake is to be alive. I have never yet met a man who was quite awake. How could I have looked him in the face?

We must learn to reawaken and keep ourselves awake, not by mechanical aids, but by an infinite expectation of the dawn, which does not forsake us in our soundest sleep. I know of no more encouraging fact than the unquestionable ability of man to elevate his life by a conscious endeavor. It is something to be able to paint a particular picture, or to carve a statue, and so to make a few objects beautiful; but it is far more glorious to carve and paint the very atmosphere and medium through which we look, which morally we can do. To affect the quality of the day, that is the highest of arts. Every man is tasked to make his life, even in its details, worthy of the contemplation of their most elevated and critical hour. If we refused, or rather used up, such paltry information as we get, the oracles would distinctly inform us how this might be done.

I went to the woods because I wished to live deliberately, to front only the essential facts of life, and see if I could not learn what it had to teach, and not, when I came to die, discover that I had not lived.

*"Mindfulness is a kind of light
that shines upon all your thoughts."*

~Thich Nhat Hanh
Going Home

28

The Universal Lyre

Sometimes, on Sundays, I heard the bells, the Lincoln, Acton, Bedford, or Concord bell, when the wind was favorable, a faint, sweet, and, as it were, natural melody, worth importing into the wilderness. At a sufficient distance over the woods this sound acquires a certain vibratory hum, as if the pine needles in the horizon were the strings of a harp which it swept. All sound heard at the greatest possible distance produces one and the same effect, a vibration of the universal lyre, just as the intervening atmosphere makes a distant ridge of earth interesting to our eyes by the azure tint it imparts to it. There came to me in this case a melody which the air had strained, and which had conversed with every leaf and needle of the wood, that portion of the sound which the elements had taken up and modulated and echoed from vale to vale. The echo is, to some extent, an original sound, and therein is the magic and charm of it. It is not merely a repetition of what was worth repeating in the bell, but partly the voice of the wood, the same trivial words and notes sung by a wood-nymph.

". . . into blue-eyed brooks that gladly
Trail their gauzy gowns and ring
Bells of glass."

~Harriet Monroe
Hetch Hetchy

29

Unfenced

To walk in a winter morning in a wood where these birds abounded, their native woods, and hear the wild cockerels crow on the trees, clear and shrill for miles over the resounding earth, drowning the feebler notes of other birds—think of it! It would put nations on the alert. Who would not be early to rise, and rise earlier and earlier every successive day of his life, till he became unspeakably healthy, wealthy, and wise? . . .

Not even a lark or an oriole, those mild plantation birds, ever visited my clearing. No cockerels to crow nor hens to cackle in the yard. No yard but unfenced nature reaching up to your very sills. A young forest growing up under your windows, and wild sumacs and blackberry vines breaking through into your cellar; sturdy pitch-pines rubbing and creaking against the shingles for want of room, their roots reaching quite under the house. Instead of a scuttle or a blind blown off in the gale, a pine tree snapped off or torn up by the roots behind your house for fuel. Instead of no path to the front-yard gate in the Great Snow, no gate—no front yard—and no path to the civilized world.

"The path of the righteous is like the light of dawn, which shines brighter and brighter until full day."

~ *Proverbs 4:18*

30

Imbibing Delight

This is a delicious evening, when the whole body is one sense, and imbibes delight through every pore. I go and come with a strange liberty in Nature, a part of herself. As I walk along the stony shore of the pond in my shirt sleeves, though it is cool as well as cloudy and windy, and I see nothing special to attract me, all the elements are unusually congenial to me. The bullfrogs trump to usher in the night, and the note of the whippoorwill is borne on the rippling wind from over the water. Sympathy with the fluttering alder and poplar leaves almost takes away my breath; yet, like the lake, my serenity is rippled but not ruffled. These small waves raised by the evening wind are as remote from storm as the smooth reflecting surface. Though it is now dark, the wind still blows and roars in the wood, the waves still dash, and some creatures lull the rest with their notes. The repose is never complete. The wildest animals do not repose, but seek their prey now; the fox, and skunk, and rabbit, now roam the fields and woods without fear. They are Nature's watchmen — links which connect the days of animated life.

"In this barrel of divine beverage are, without fail, several taps."

~ Marguerite Porete
Mirror of Simple Souls

31

Something Kindred

There can be no very black melancholy to him who lives in the midst of Nature and has his senses still. . . . I have never felt lonesome, or in the least oppressed by a sense of solitude, but once, and that was a few weeks after I came to the woods, when, for an hour, I doubted if the near neighborhood of men was not essential to a serene and healthy life. To be alone was something unpleasant. But I was at the same time conscious of a slight insanity in my mood, and seemed to foresee my recovery. In the midst of a gentle rain while these thoughts prevailed, I was suddenly sensible of such sweet and beneficent society in Nature, in the very pattering of the drops, and in every sound and sight around my house, an infinite and unaccountable friendliness all at once like an atmosphere sustaining me, as made the fancied advantages of human neighborhood insignificant, and I have never thought of them since. Every little pine needle expanded and swelled with sympathy and befriended me. I was so distinctly made aware of the presence of something kindred to me, even in scenes which we are accustomed to call wild and dreary, and also that the nearest of blood to me and humanest was not a person nor a villager, that I thought no place could ever be strange to me again.

"Praised be You, my Lord, through Sister Water."

~ Francis of Assisi
from *Classics of Spirituality*

32

Entertainment

The nighthawk circled overhead in the sunny afternoon—for I sometimes made a day of it—like a mote in the eye, or in heaven's eye, falling from time to time with a swoop and a sound as if the heavens were rent, torn at last to very rags and tatters, and yet a seamless cope remained; small imps that fill the air and lay their eggs on the ground on bare sand or rocks on the tops of hills, where few have found them; graceful and slender like ripples caught up from the pond, as leaves are raised by the wind to float in the heavens; such kindredship is in Nature. The hawk is aerial brother of the wave which he sails over and surveys, those his perfect air-inflated wings answering to the elemental unfledged pinions of the sea. Or sometimes I watched a pair of hen-hawks circling high in the sky, alternately soaring and descending, approaching and leaving one another, as if they were the embodiment of my own thoughts. Or I was attracted by the passage of wild pigeons from this wood to that, with a slight quivering winnowing sound and carrier haste; or from under a rotten stump my hoe turned up a sluggish, portentous, and outlandish spotted salamander, a trace of Egypt and the Nile, yet our contemporary. When I paused to lean on my hoe, these sounds and sights I heard and saw anywhere in the row, a part of the inexhaustible entertainment which the country offers.

*"In the wing of a fly, an ocean of wonder;
in the pupil of the eye, an endless heaven."*

~ Mahmud Shabistari
quoted by Jonathan Star in *Two Suns Rising*

33

Lost

It is a surprising and memorable, as well as valuable experience, to be lost in the woods any time. Often in a snowstorm, even by day, one will come out upon a well-known road and yet find it impossible to tell which way leads to the village. Though he knows that he has traveled it a thousand times, he cannot recognize a feature in it, but it is as strange to him as if it were a road in Siberia. By night, of course, the perplexity is infinitely greater. In our most trivial walks, we are constantly, though unconsciously, steering like pilots by certain well-known beacons and headlands, and if we go beyond our usual course we still carry in our minds the bearing of some neighboring cape; and not till we are completely lost, or turned round—for he needs only to be turned round once with eyes shut in this world to be lost—do we appreciate the vastness and strangeness of Nature. Every man has to learn the points of compass again as often as he awakes, whether from sleep or any abstraction. Not till we are lost, in other words, not till we have lost the world, do we begin to find ourselves, and realize where we are and the infinite extent of our relations.

*"The one who finds his life will lose it,
and the one who loses his life for my sake will find it."*

~ Jesus
Matthew 10:39

34

Earth's Eye

The forest has never so good a setting, nor is so distinctly beautiful, as when seen from the middle of a small lake amid hills which rise from the water's edge; for the water in which it is reflected not only makes the best foreground in such a case, but, with its winding shore, the most natural and agreeable boundary to it. There is no rawness nor imperfection in its edge there, as where the axe has cleared a part, or a cultivated field abuts on it. The trees have ample room to expand on the water side, and each sends forth its most vigorous branch in that direction. There Nature has woven a natural selvage, and the eye rises by just gradations from the low shrubs of the shore to the highest trees. There are few traces of man hands to be seen. The water laves the shore as it did a thousand years ago.

A lake is the landscape's most beautiful and expressive feature. It is earth's eye; looking into which the beholder measures the depth of his own nature. The fluviatile trees next the shore are the slender eyelashes which fringe it, and the wooded hills and cliffs around are its overhanging brows.

> *"My daily meditations inside this weather-beaten studio are most often centered on water."*

~ Brenda Peterson
Singing the Sound

35

Dreaming the Wind

It was as if we sucked at the very teats of Nature's pine-clad bosom in these parts—the sap of all Millinocket botany commingled—the topmost, most fantastic, and spiciest sprays of the primitive wood, and whatever invigorating and stringent gum or essence it afforded steeped and dissolved in it—a lumberer's drink, which would acclimate and naturalize a man at once—which would make him see green, and, if he slept, dream that he heard the wind sough among the pines. Here was a fife, praying to be played on, through which we breathed a few tuneful strains—brought hither to tame wild beasts.

*"Through the empty branches
the sky remains.
It is what you have.
Be earth now, and evensong.
Be the ground lying under that sky."*

~ Rainer Maria Rilke
"You are not surprised at the force of the storm"

36

A Night in the Woods

We hastily drew up the batteau just within the edge of the woods before the fire, and. . . spread the tent on the ground to lie on; and with the corner of a blanket, or what more or less we could get to put over us, lay down with our heads and bodies under the boat, and our feet and legs on the sand toward the fire. At first we lay awake, talking of our course, and finding ourselves in so convenient a posture for studying the heavens, with the moon and stars shining in our faces, our conversation naturally turned upon astronomy, and we recounted by turns the most interesting discoveries in that science. But at length we composed ourselves seriously to sleep. . . . Thus aroused [at midnight], I too brought fresh fuel to the fire, and then rambled along the sandy shore in the moonlight, hoping to meet a moose, come down to drink, or else a wolf. The little rill tinkled the louder, and peopled all the wilderness for me; and the glassy smoothness of the sleeping lake, laving the shores of a new world, with the dark, fantastic rocks rising here and there from its surface, made a scene not easily described. It has left such an impression of stern, yet gentle, wildness on my memory as will not soon be effaced.

"We have begun our engagement with a place,
a place defined by the waters of the river we work in,
a place where we may yet come to be at home."

~ Freeman House
Totem Salmon

37

Edging Toward the Clouds

In the morning, after whetting our appetite on some raw pork, a wafer of hard bread, and a dipper of condensed cloud or waterspout, we all together began to make our way up the falls, which I have described; this time choosing the right hand, or highest peak, which was not the one I had approached before. But soon my companions were lost to my sight behind the mountain ridge in my rear, which still seemed ever retreating before me, and I climbed alone over huge rocks, loosely poised, a mile or more, still edging toward the clouds—for though the day was clear elsewhere, the summit was concealed by mist. The mountain seemed a vast aggregation of loose rocks, as if some time it had rained rocks, and they lay as they fell on the mountain sides, nowhere fairly at rest, but leaning on each other, all rocking-stones, with cavities between, but scarcely any soil or smoother shelf. They were the raw materials of a planet dropped from an unseen quarry, which the vast chemistry of nature would anon work up or work down, into the smiling and verdant plains and valleys of earth. This was an undone extremity of the globe; as in lignite, we see coal in the process of formation.

At length I entered within the skirts of the cloud which seemed forever drifting over the summit. . . . Sometimes it seemed as if the summit would be cleared in a few moments, and smile in sunshine:

but what was gained on one side was lost on another. It was like sitting in a chimney and waiting for the smoke to blow away. It was, in fact, a cloud-factory—these were the cloud-works, and the wind turned them off done from the cool, bare rocks.

"The Master allows things to come and go.
The sage's heart is open as the sky."

~ Lao Tzu
The Tao, translated by Stephen Mitchell

38

Amid the Howling of Wolves

Thus a man shall lead his life away here on the edge of the wilderness, on Indian Millinocket stream, in a new world, far in the dark of the continent, and have a flute to play at evening here, while his strains echo to the stars, amid the howling of wolves; shall live, as it were, in the primitive age of the world, a primitive man. Yet one shall spend a sunny day, and in this century be my contemporary; perchance shall read some scattered leaves of literature, and sometimes talk with me. Why read history, then, if the ages and the generations are now? One lives three thousand years deep into time, an age not yet described by poets. Can you well go further back in history than this? Ay! Ay!—for there turns up but now into the mouth of Millinocket stream a still more ancient and primitive man, whose history is not brought down even to the former. In a bark vessel sewn with the roots of the spruce, with horn-beam paddles, he dips his way along. He is but dim and misty to me, obscured by the aeons that lie between the bark-canoe and the batteau. He builds no house of logs, but a wigwam of skins. He eats no hot-bread and sweet-cake, but musquash and moose-meat and the fat of bears.

He glides up the Millinocket and is lost to my sight, as a more distant and misty cloud is seen flitting by behind a nearer, and is lost in space.

"When I am invaded by Immanence,
most often in the presence of beauty or love or relief,
my response is to open myself to its blessing."

~ Ursula Goodenough
The Sacred Depths of Nature

39

The Seasons in You

To insure health, a man's relation to Nature must come very near to a personal one; he must be conscious of a friendliness in her; when human friends fail or die, she must stand in the gap to him. I cannot conceive of any life which deserves the name, unless there is a certain tender relation to Nature. This it is which makes winter warm, and supplies society in the desert and wilderness. Unless Nature sympathizes with and speaks to us, as it were, the most fertile and blooming regions are barren and dreary. . . .

I do not see that I can live tolerably without affection for Nature. If I feel no softening toward the rocks, what do they signify?

I do not think much of that chemistry that can extract corn and potatoes out of a barren, but rather of that chemistry that can extract thoughts and sentiments out of the life of a man on any soil. It is in vain to write on the seasons unless you have the seasons in you.

"*God created nights, seasons, lunar days, and week days,*
Wind, water, fire, and the nether regions.
In the midst of these God established the earth as a temple."

~ The Japji, Sikh scripture
Sacred Writings

40

At Home Everywhere

I have met with but one or two persons in the
course of my life who understood the art of
Walking, that is, of taking walks—who had a genius,
so to speak, for *sauntering*: which word is beautifully
derived "from idle people who roved about the
country, in the Middle Ages, and asked charity,
under pretense of going *à la Sainte Terre*, to the Holy
Land, till the children exclaimed, 'There goes a *Sainte-
Terrer*,'" a Saunterer, a Holy-Lander. They who never
go to the Holy Land in their walks, as they pretend,
are indeed mere idlers and vagabonds; but they who
do go there are saunterers in the good sense, such as
I mean. Some, however, would derive the word from
sans terre, without land or a home, which, therefore,
in the good sense, will mean, having no particular
home, but equally at home everywhere. For this is
the secret of successful sauntering.

He who sits still in a house all the time may be
the greatest vagrant of all; but the saunterer, in the
good sense, is no more vagrant than the meandering
river which is all the while sedulously seeking the
shortest course to the sea. But I prefer the first,
which indeed, is the most probable derivation. For
every walk is a sort of crusade, preached by some
Peter the Hermit in us, to go forth and reconquer
this Holy Land from the hands of the Infidels. . . .

So we saunter toward the Holy Land, till one day the sun shall shine more brightly than ever he has done, shall perchance shine into our minds and hearts, and light up our whole lives with a great awakening light, as warm and serene and golden as on a bankside in autumn.

*"In silent wonder the wise see the Creator
as the life flaming in all creation."*

~ Mundaka Upanishad
The Upanishads

41

Legs

No wealth can buy the requisite leisure, freedom, and independence which are the capital in this profession. It comes only by the grace of God. It requires a direct dispensation from Heaven to become a walker. You must be born into the family of the Walkers. . . .

I think that I cannot preserve my health and spirits, unless I spend four hours a day at least— and it is commonly more than that—sauntering through the woods and over the hills and fields, absolutely free from all worldly engagements. You may safely say, A penny for your thoughts, or a thousand pounds. When sometimes I am reminded that the mechanics and shopkeepers stay in their shops not only all the forenoon, but all the afternoon too, sitting with crossed legs, so many of them —as if the legs were made to sit upon, and not to stand or walk upon—I think that they deserve some credit for not having all committed suicide long ago.

*"It is always worth while to sit or
kneel at the feet of grandeur."*

~ John Burroughs
Divine Abyss

42

Springs of Life

But the walking of which I speak has nothing in it akin to taking exercise, as it is called, as the sick take medicine at stated hours—as the swinging of dumbbells or chairs; but is itself the enterprise and adventure of the day. If you would get exercise, go in search of the springs of life. Think of a man's swinging dumbbells for his health, when those springs are bubbling up in far-off pastures unsought by them!

Moreover, you must walk like a camel, which is said to be the only beast which ruminates when walking. When a traveler asked Wordsworth's servant to show him her master's study, she answered, "Here is his library, but his study is out of doors."

Living much out of doors, in the sun and wind, will no doubt produce a certain roughness of character—will cause a thicker cuticle to grow over some of the finer qualities of our nature, as on the face and hands, or as severe manual labor robs the hands of some of their delicacy of touch. . . . There will be so much the more air and sunshine in our thoughts.

*"O happy living things! no tongue
Their beauty might declare:
A spring of love gushed from my heart,
And I blessed them unaware."*

~ Samuel Taylor Coleridge
"The Rime of the Ancient Mariner"

43

The Woods Within

When we walk, we naturally go to the fields and woods: what would become of us, if we walked only in a garden or a mall? Even some sects of philosophers have felt the necessity of importing the woods to themselves, since they did not go to the woods. "They planted groves and walks of Platanes," where they took *subdiales ambulationes* in porticos open to the air. Of course it is of no use to direct our steps to the woods, if they do not carry us thither. I am alarmed when it happens that I have walked a mile into the woods bodily, without getting there in spirit. In my afternoon walk I would fain forget all my morning occupations and my obligations to society. But it sometimes happens that I cannot easily shake off the village. The thought of some work will run in my head and I am not where my body is—I am out of my senses. In my walks I would fain return to my senses. What business have I in the woods, if I am thinking of something out of the woods?

"If a person does not see, hear, or smell
civilization, he or she is in wilderness."

~ Roderick Frazier Nash
Wilderness and the American Mind

44

Horse Country

Some do not walk at all; others walk in the high-ways; a few walk across lots. Roads are made for horses and men of business. I do not travel in them much, comparatively, because I am not in a hurry to get to any tavern or grocery or livery-stable or depot to which they lead. I am a good horse to travel, but not from choice a roadster. The landscape-painter uses the figures of men to mark a road. He would not make that use of my figure. I walk out into a nature such as the old prophets and poets, Menu, Moses, Homer, Chaucer, walked in. You may name it America, but it is not America; neither Americus Vespucius, nor Columbus, nor the rest were the dis-coverers of it. There is a truer account of it in myth-ology than in any history of America, so called, that I have seen. . . .

What is it that makes it so hard sometimes to determine whither we will walk? I believe that there is a subtle magnetism in Nature, which, if we un-consciously yield to it, will direct us aright.

*"A man may be a poor, inferior creature,
yet when he speaks there is in those words
all the wisdom in the world."*

~ Homer
The Odyssey

45

Wild Tea

The West of which I speak is but another name for the Wild; and what I have been preparing to say is, that in Wildness is the preservation of the World. Every tree sends its fibers forth in search of the Wild. The cities import it at any price. Men plow and sail for it. From the forest and wilderness come the tonics and barks which brace mankind. . . .

I believe in the forest, and in the meadow, and in the night in which the corn grows. We require an infusion of hemlock, spruce or arbor vitae in our tea. . . .

Life consists with wildness. The most alive is the wildest. Not yet subdued by man, its presence refreshes him.

"God leads this spirit into a desert
into the wilderness and solitude of the divinity. . .
where God gushes up within."

~ Meister Eckhart
quoted by Andrew Harvey in *The Essential Mystics*

46

When I Would Recreate Myself

When I would recreate myself, I seek the darkest wood, the thickest and most interminable and, to the citizen, most dismal, swamp. I enter a swamp as a sacred place, a *sanctum sanctorum*. There is the strength, the marrow, of Nature. The wildwood covers the virgin mould, and the same soil is good for men and for trees. A man's health requires as many acres of meadow to his prospect as his farm does loads of muck. There are the strong meats on which they feed. A town is saved, not more by the righteous men in it than by the woods and swamps that surround it. A township where one primitive forest waves above while another primitive forest rots below—such a town is fitted to raise not only corn and potatoes, but poets and philosophers for the coming ages. In such a soil grew Homer and Confucius and the rest, and out of such a wilderness comes the Reformer eating locusts and wild honey.

"Recite in the name of Allah,
who created humans from clots of blood."

~ Qur'an
Surah 96:1

47

Unto a Life

Unto a life which I call natural I would gladly follow even a will-o'-the-wisp through bogs and sloughs unimaginable, but no moon nor firefly has shown me the causeway to it. Nature is a personality so vast and universal that we have never seen one of her features. The walker in the familiar fields which stretch around my native town sometimes finds himself in another land than is described in their owners' deeds, as it were in some far-away field on the confines of the actual Concord, where her jurisdiction ceases, and the idea which the word Concord suggests ceases to be suggested. These farms which I have myself surveyed, these bounds which I have set up, appear dimly still as through a mist; but they have no chemistry to fix them; they fade from the surface of the glass, and the picture which the painter painted stands out dimly from beneath. The world with which we are commonly acquainted leaves no trace, and it will have no anniversary.

"When someone asks what there is to do,
light the candle in their hand.
Like this."

~ Rumi
"Like This"

48

Mount the Earth

We hug the earth—how rarely we mount! Methinks we might elevate ourselves a little more. We might climb a tree, at least. I found my account in climbing a tree once. It was a tall white-pine, on the top of a hill; and though I got well pitched, I was well paid for it, for I discovered new mountains in the horizon which I had never seen before—so much more of the earth and the heavens. I might have walked about the foot of the tree for threescore years and ten, and yet I certainly should never have seen them. But, above all, I discovered around me—it was near the end of June—on the ends of the topmost branches only, a few minute and delicate red cone-like blossoms, the fertile flower of the white pine looking heavenward. I carried straightway to the village the topmost spire, and showed it to stranger jury-men who walked the streets—for it was court week—and to farmers and lumber-dealers and wood-choppers and hunters, and not one had ever seen the like before, but they wondered as at a star dropped down. Tell of ancient architects finishing their works on the tops of columns as perfectly as on the lower and more visible parts! Nature has from the first expanded the minute blossoms of the forest only toward the heavens, above men's heads and unobserved by them.

We see only the flowers that are under our feet in the meadows. The pines have developed their delicate blossoms on the highest twigs of the wood every summer for ages, as well over the heads of Nature's red children as of her white ones; yet scarcely a farmer or hunter in the land has ever seen them.

" 'Go to the trees,' the old one told me
'Ask them where they find their strength
And you will find your answer.' "

~ Sharron Johnstone, Cree nation
Spirit Songs

49

God's Lurking Places

The art of spending a day! If it is possible that we may be addressed, it behooves us to be attentive. If by watching all day and all night, I may detect some trace of the Ineffable, then will it not be worth the while to watch? Watch and pray without ceasing?. . .

If by watching a whole year on the city's walls I may obtain a communication from heaven, shall I not do well to shut up my shop and turn a watchman? Can a youth, a man, do more wisely than to go where his life is to be found? As if I had suffered that to be rumor which may be verified. We are surrounded by a rich and fertile mystery. May we not probe it, pry into it, employ ourselves about it—a little? To devote your life to the discovery of the divinity in Nature or to the eating of oysters: would they not be attended with very different results? . . .

To watch for, describe, all the divine features which I detect in Nature.

My profession is to be always on the alert to find God in nature—to know His lurking places.

*"Fear is not a bad place to start
a spiritual journey."*

~ Kathleen Norris
Dakota

50

By Their Flowers

Moralists say of men, "By their fruits ye shall know them," but botanists have commonly said of plants, "By their flowers ye shall know them." This is very well generally, but they should make an exception when the *fruit* is fairer than the flower. They are to be compared at that stage when they are most significant to man. I say that sometimes by their fruits ye shall know them, though I here use the word *fruit* in the popular sense.

It may be worth the while to consider for a moment what a fruit is. The mystery of the life of plants is kindred with that of our own lives, and the physiologist must not be in too much haste to explain their growth according to mechanical laws, or as he might explain some machinery of his own making. We must not presume to probe with our fingers the sanctuary of any life, whether animal or vegetable; if we do we shall discover nothing but surface still, or all fruits will be apples of the Dead Sea, full of dust and ashes.

. . . the essence is (so to speak) as far on the other side of the surface (or matter) as reverence detains the worshipper on this, and only reverence can find out this angle. Shall we presume to alter the angle at which the Maker chooses to be seen?

"We are speaking of things that are barely visible —
of the most intimate and fragile things,
of flowers that open only in the night."

~ Carl Jung
The Spiritual Problem of Modern Man

51

Sweet Scent of the Earth

I perceive from time to time in the spring and have long kept a record of it, an indescribably sweet fragrance, which I cannot trace to any particular source. It is, perchance, that sweet scent of the earth of which the ancients speak. Though I have not detected the flower that emits it, this appears to be its fruit. It is natural that the first fruit which the earth bears should emit and be, as it were, a concentration and embodiment of that vernal fragrance with which the air has lately teemed. Strawberries are the manna found, ere long, where that fragrance has been. Are not the juices of each fruit distilled from the air?

This is one of the fruits as remarkable for its fragrance as its flavor, and it is said to have got its Latin name, *fraga*, from this fact. Its fragrance, like that of the checkerberry, is a very prevalent one. Wilted young twigs of several evergreens, especially the fir-balsam, smell very much like it.

Only one in a hundred know where to look for these early strawberries. It is, as it were, a sort of Indian knowledge acquired by secret tradition.

"There is no one who does not eat and drink,
but there are few who can really know flavor."

~ Confucius
Chung Yung

52

Your Real Garden

There is no wilder and richer sight than is afforded from such a point of view of the edge of a blueberry swamp, when various wild berries are intermixed.

There was Charles Miles's Swamp also, where you might get more than the value of the berries in the beauty of the spruce trees with which it was beset, though not the less wildly rich and beautiful—the cool blueberries hung high over your head there. I remember years ago picking blueberries in that swamp, before it began to be *redeemed*, when from its very depths I could hear the trembling strains of Mr. Miles's bass viol, from the unseen house, for he was a famous timist and held the choir to harmony on the sabbath. I am not sure but some echo of those strains "touched my trembling ears" and reminded me about those times what true fame was, for it did not seem a "mortal soil" where I stood.

Thus, any summer, after spending the forenoon in your chamber reading or writing, in the afternoon you walk forth into the fields and woods, and turn aside, if you please, into some rich, withdrawn, and untrodden swamp, and find there bilberries large and fair awaiting you in inexhaustible abundance. This is your real garden.

"They heard the sound of the LORD God walking in the garden at the time of the evening breeze."

~ Genesis 3:8

53

Huckleberry University

These berries are further important as introducing children to the fields and woods. The season of berrying is so far respected that the school children have a vacation then, and many little fingers are busy picking these small fruits. It is even a pastime, not a drudgery, though it often pays well beside. . . .

I served my apprenticeship and have since done considerable journeywork in the huckleberry field. Though I never paid for my schooling and clothing in that way, it was some of the best schooling that I got, and paid for itself. Theodore Parker is not the only New England boy who has got his education by picking huckleberries, though he may not have gone to Harvard thereafter nor to any school more distant than the huckleberry field. *There* was a university itself, where you could learn the everlasting Laws and Medicine and Theology, not under Story and Warren and Ware, but far wiser professors than they. Why such haste to go from the huckleberry field to the college yard?

As in old times, they who dwelt on the heath, remote from towns , being backward to adopt the doctrines which prevailed in towns, were called "heathen" in a bad sense, so I trust that we dwellers in the huckleberry pastures, which are our heath-lands, shall be slow to adopt the notions of large towns and cities, though perchance we may be nick-named "huckleberry people."

"I do not know what I may appear to the world; but to myself I seem to have been only a boy playing on the seashore."

~ Sir Isaac Newton
Memoirs of Newton

54

Native Americans

I state this to show how contented and thankful we ought to be.

It is to be remembered that the vegetation in Great Britain is that of a much more northern latitude than where we live, that some of our alpine shrubs are found on the plain there; and their two whortleberries are alpine or extreme northern plants with us.

If you look closely you will find blueberry and huckleberry bushes under your feet, though they may be feeble and barren, throughout all our woods, the most persevering Native Americans, ready to shoot up into place and power at the next election among the plants, ready to reclothe the hills when man has laid them bare and feed all kinds of pensioners. What though the woods be cut down; it appears that this emergency was long ago anticipated and provided for by Nature, and the interregnum is not allowed to be a barren one. She not only begins instantly to heal that scar, but she compensates us for the loss and refreshes us with fruits such as the forest did not produce. As the sandal wood is said to diffuse a perfume around the woodcutter who cuts it, so in this case Nature rewards with unexpected fruits the hand that lays her waste.

"Unless you respect the earth, you destroy it."

~ Oren Lyons, Onondaga chief
Wisdomkeepers

55

Wild Like Myself

When I go by this shrub thus late and hardy, and see its dangling fruit, I respect the tree, and I am grateful for Nature's bounty, even though I cannot eat it. Here on this rugged and woody hillside has grown an apple tree, not planted by man, no relic of a former orchard, but a natural growth, like the pines and oaks. Most fruits which we prize and use depend entirely on our care. Corn and grain, potatoes, peaches, melons, and so on, depend altogether on our planting; but the apple emulates man's independence and enterprise. It is not simply carried but, like him, to some extent, it has migrated to this New World and is even, here and there, making its way amid the aboriginal trees, just as the ox and dog and horse sometimes run wild and maintain themselves.

Even the sourest and crabbedest apple growing in the most unfavorable position suggests such thoughts as these, it is so noble a fruit.

Nevertheless, *our* wild apple is wild only like myself, perchance, who belong not to the aboriginal race here, but have strayed into the woods from the cultivated stock.

"*Then I remember, surprised I could have ever forgotten,
that I am a part of everything and everything is a part of me.
Our identities are inseparable.*"

~ Baxter Trautman
Spirit of the Valley

56

Symbol of Fertility

We love to see Nature fruitful in whatever kind. It assures us of her vigor and that she may in equal profusion bring forth the fruits which we prize. I love to see the acorns plenty even in the shrub oaks. I love to see the potato balls numerous and large as I go through the low fields, poisonous though they look—the plant thus, as it were, bearing fruit at both ends—as much as to say, I offer you not only these tubers for the present, but, if they do not satisfy you, and you will have new varieties, plant these seeds. What bounty—what beauty even! These balls which are worthless to the farmer combine to make the general impression of the year's fruitfulness. It is as cheering to me as the rapid increase of the population of New York. One of these drooping clusters of potato balls would be as good a symbol of our year's fertility as anything I know of—better as yet, surely, than a bunch of grapes.

"As a person awakens to a sense of universal unification, everything glows as if impregnated."

~ Thomas Aquinas
quoted by Sigurd Olson in *Open Horizons*

57

Ripeness

There is no ripeness which is not, so to speak, something ultimate in itself, and not merely a perfected means to what we believe to be a higher end. In order to be ripe it must serve a transcendent use. The ripeness of a leaf being perfected (for aught we know), it leaves the tree at that point and never returns to it. It has nothing to do with any other fruit which the tree may bear, and only genius can pluck it. The fruit of a tree is neither in the seed, nor the timber—nor is it the full-grown tree itself—but I would prefer to consider it for the present as simply the highest use to which it can be put. As Mrs. Lincoln says in her *Botany*, "The maturity of the seed marks the close of the life of annual plants, and the suspension of vegetation in woody and perennial ones."

When La Mountain and Haddock dropped down into the Canada wilderness the other day, they came near starving or dying of cold, wet, and fatigue, not knowing where to look for food nor how to shelter themselves. Thus far we have wandered from a simple and independent life. I think that a wise and independent, self-reliant man will have a complete list of the edibles to be found in a primitive country or wilderness—a bill of fare in their waistcoat pocket, at least, to say nothing of matches and warm clothing, so that he can commence a systematic search for them without loss of time. They might have had several frogs a piece if they had known how to find them. . . . Why, a merely aesthetic philosopher, who soars higher than usual in his thoughts, from time to time drops down into what is just such a wilderness to him as that was to La Mountain and Haddock, where he finds scarcely one little frog gone into winter quarters, to sustain himself, and runs screaming toward the climes of the sun.

"The vine withers,
the fig tree droops.
Pomegranate, palm, and apple—
all the trees of the field are dried up;
surely, joy withers away
among the people."

~ The Prophet Joel
Joel 1:12

58

Sunlight, Icelight

It is as if all the rays slid over the ice and lodged against and were reflected by the stubble. It is surprising how much sunny light a little straw that survives the winter will reflect.

The channel of the river is open part of the way. The *Cornus sericea* and some quite young willow shoots are the red-barked twigs so conspicuous now along the riversides.

That bright and warm reflection of sunlight from the insignificant edging of stubble was remarkable. I was coming downstream over the meadows, on the ice, within four or five rods of the eastern shore. The sun on my left was about a quarter of an hour above the horizon. The ice was soft and sodden, of a dull lead-color, quite dark and reflecting no light as I looked eastward, but my eyes caught by accident a singular sunny brightness reflected from the narrow border of stubble only three or four inches high (and as many feet wide perhaps) which rose along the edge of the ice at the foot of the hill. It was not a mere brightening of the bleached stubble, but the warm and yellow light of the sun, which, it appeared, it was peculiarly fitted to reflect. It was that amber light from the west which we sometimes witness after a storm, concentrated on this stubble, for the hill beyond was merely a dark russet spotted with snow. All the yellow rays seemed to be reflected by this insignificant stubble alone, and when I looked more generally a little above it, seeing it with the under part of my eye, it appeared yet more truly and more bright; the reflected light made its due impression on my eye, separated from the proper color of the stubble, and it glowed almost like a low, steady, and serene fire. It was precisely as if the sunlight had mechanically slid over the ice, and lodged against the stubble. It will be enough to say of something warmly and sunnily bright that it glowed like lit stubble. It was remarkable that, looking eastward, this was the only evidence of the light in the west.

*"I tried to prove that the never ending search
for the essence of the wild was the
underlying motive of all trips and expeditions."*

~ Sigurd Olson
Open Horizons

59

Nature's Prescription

Live in each season as it passes; breathe the air,
drink the drink, taste the fruit, and resign yourself to the influences of each. Let these be your only
diet-drink and botanical medicines. In August live
on berries, not dried meats and pemmican, as if you
were on shipboard making your way through a
waste ocean or on the Darien Grounds. Be blown on
by all the winds. Open all your pores and bathe in
all the tides of nature, in all her streams and oceans,
at all seasons. Miasma and infection are from within, not without. The invalid brought to the brink of
the grave by an unnatural life, instead of imbibing
the great influence that Nature is, drinks only of the
tea made of a particular herb, while he still contin-
ues his unnatural life—saves at the spile and wastes
at the bung. He does not love Nature or his life, and
so sickens and dies, and no doctor can cure him.
Grow green with spring, yellow and ripe with
autumn. Drink of each season's influence as a vial, a
true panacea of all remedies mixed for your especial
use. The vials of summer never made a man sick,
only those which he had stored in his cellar. Drink
the wines, not of your own, but of Nature's bottling
—not kept in a goat– or pig-skin, but in the skin of a
myriad fair berries. Let Nature do your bottling, as
also your pickling and preserving. For all Nature is
doing her best each moment to make us well. She
exists for no other end. Do not resist her. With the
least inclination to be well, we should not be sick.

Men have discovered, or think that they have discovered, the salutariness of a few wild things only,
and not of all Nature. Why, Nature is but another
name for health.

"The larger the island of knowledge,
the longer the shoreline of wonder."

~ Huston Smith
The World's Religions

60

A Budding Ecstasy

Hermit alone. Let me see; where was I? Methinks I was nearly in this frame of mind; the world lay about at this angle. Shall I go to heaven or a-fishing? If I should soon bring this meditation to an end, would another so sweet occasion be likely to offer? I was as near being resolved into the essence of things as ever I was in my life. I fear my thoughts will not come back to me. If it would do any good, I would whistle for them. When they make us an offer, is it wise to say, We will think of it? My thoughts have left no track, and I cannot find the path again. What was it that I was thinking of? It was a very hazy day. I will just try these three sentences of Confucius; they may fetch that state about again. I know not whether it was the dumps or a budding ecstasy.

"When it's over, I want to say:
all my life
I was a bride married to amazement."

~ Mary Oliver
"When Death Comes"

"Take all away from me, But leave me ecstasy."

~ Emily Dickinson
quoted in Dorothee Soelle, *The Silent Cry*

Afterword

Still will I strive to be
As if thou wert with me;
Whatever path I take,
It shall be for thy sake,
Of gentle slope and wide,
As thou wert by my side,
Without a root
To trip thy gentle foot.

I'll walk with gentle pace,
And choose the smoothest place,
And careful dip the oar,
And shun the winding shore,
And gently steer my boat
Where water-lilies float,
And cardinal flowers
Stand in their sylvan bowers.

~ Henry David Thoreau
from *"Low in the Eastern Sky"*

Sources

In the preceding text the source of each Thoreau quote is identified by a particular leaf icon, shown following the passage. Below is a key to those sources:

 Walden

 A Winter Walk

 Civil Disobedience

 The Maine Woods

 A Week on the Concord and Merrimack Rivers

 A Yankee in Canada

 Journal

Walking

 Wild Fruits

Backwoods and along the Seashore
>   Edited by Peter Turner. Boston:
>   Shambhala. 1995. Selections from *The
>   Maine Woods* and *Cape Cod*.

The Portable Thoreau
>   Edited by Carl Bode. N.Y.: Viking. 1977.
>   The volume includes: *A Winter Walk*; *Civil
>   Disobedience*; *A Week on the Concord and
>   Merrimack Rivers*; *A Yankee in Canada*; *Walden*;
>   *Journal*; and, *Walking*.

The Writings of Ralph Waldo Emerson
>   Edited by Brooks Atkinson. N.Y.: Random
>   House. 1950. Thoreau (1862 Eulogy)

Wild Fruits
>   Edited by Bradley Dean. N.Y.: W.W.
>   Norton. 2001.

Acknowledgments

The author wishes to express gratitude and appreciation to the following:

Bradley Dean of the Thoreau Society for prompt permission to use excerpts from his collection of Wild Fruits;

Mike Jones, publisher, for sauntering into new publishing territory with this series;

Gene and Nell Arntz who supported my first venture into self-publishing that led to the meditation books;

Mia Monroe, head interpretive ranger at Muir Woods National Monument, and David Blackburn, ranger at the John Muir Historic Site in Martinez, California, for their enthusiastic encouragement;

My good friends on many a hiking path: Todd Jolly, Heather Voss and Carol Hovis for all the exploring by temple light, snowshoes, tree-climbs, and tea-sharing moments over Svea stoves;

Seido Lee deBarros of Green Gulch Zen Farm for friendship along the trails of breath and awareness.

Meditations of Henry David Thoreau: A Light in the Woods was created on a Power Macintosh G3, using QuarkXpress 4.1 and Adobe Photoshop 5.5. The text and display font is Bitstream's *Calligraphic 810*; the "leaf" icons belong to Andrew D. Taylor's *ArborisFolium*; and the "book" and "spiral" graphics belong to P22's *Arts and Crafts Ornaments 2*.

Photo Credits

Chris Highland is an interspiritual chaplain, author, songwriter and poet. He completed his under-graduate studies in religion and philosophy in Seattle, Washington before settling in the San Francisco Bay Area to complete his Masters degree. A passionate saunterer, he enjoys an intimate relation with Nature in forests, mountains and water-falls. An avowed heretic ("one who seeks new paths"), Chris' writing reflects his exploration of the edges of human society and his playful search for what Emerson called "high, clear and spiritual conversation," to be had by each and every one of us as "beggars on the highway."

Chris is the author of *Meditations of John Muir: Nature's Temple*, *Meditations of Walt Whitman: Earth, My Likeness*, and *Meditations of Ralph Waldo Emerson: Into the Green Future*, all from Wilderness Press. An eclectic map of Chris' creative thought and colorful photography can be read and seen at www.naturetemple.net.

More meditations…

Meditations of
John Muir:
Nature's Temple

Insightful quotations from America's preeminent naturalist, writer, and activist are paired with selections from other cele- brated thinkers and spiritual texts.

ISBN 0-89997-285-3

Meditations of
Walt Whitman:
Earth, My Likeness

Contains 60 passages from Whitman's great planting of poems, Leaves of Grass, compiled over a lifetime spanning nearly the entire 19th century, plus complementary quotes from others.

ISBN 0-89997-362-0

Meditations of
Ralph Waldo Emerson:
Into the Green Future

Selections from 30 years of Emerson's writings reveal the essence of this great author, poet and philosopher, along with quota- tions from historical and contemporary thinkers.

ISBN 0-89997-352-3